Things I Can't Say

Brianna Nielson

BookLeaf Publishing

India | USA | UK

Things I Can't Say © 2022

Brianna Nielson

All rights reserved.

Presentation by *BookLeaf Publishing*

Web: www.bookleafpub.com

E-mail: info@bookleafpub.com

ISBN: 978-93-5744-701-0

First edition 2022

DEDICATION

For anyone that ever heard me

and anyone that ever will

PREFACE

This is a collection of thoughts, of feelings, or words that I found while I was walking through life. Like the rocks and leaves trailed in after a frolic in the woods, these are my precious messes. The clumps of dirt I saw shapes in, the bugs I named and made into pets. This is my first collection of poetry.

- Brianna

Good Morning Love

You were late, as usual
I didn't hold it against you
not like you hold me.
Almost used the flyswatter as a spatula
when I flipped your pancakes though.
After we kissed I could
still taste you and the powdered sugar,
which kept me high
all through the day.
Good morning love
like good morning breath.
Good morning and
good mourning
for my past spent without you

Sex and the City

Living in the city is sexy

So many eyes caressing your skin
it's like I'm a pole dancer at 18

The rumble of the bike engine passing by makes
my hips sway a little deeper

Neon lights changing in the night
drugging me up with no needle

Living in the city is sexy

Black shiny leather tights
sparkling under headlights

Drooling fangs and predator minds
like being hunted is seductive

On a knife's edge balanced like a top
Until something pushes me over

Living in the City is Sexy

Villain

Why does it sound like your voice every time I
hear a breakup song on the radio

Like you're reaching across the cosmos to
remind me what I did to you

Why don't we write songs about the broken
heartbreakers

The ones that didn't want to play the villain
But had to

Monster

Disfigured and twisted

She lurks in the dark

Vile and repulsive

She sits on my heart

Quiet and careful

She whispers her thoughts

Gnarled and hardened

Her fingers twist knots

Persistent and still

She waits for her moment

Vulnerable and hurt

She strikes on the beat

Sorry and violent

She makes me unmade

My monster's not me
But I am my monster

Nothing Sometimes

I just feel nothing sometimes
And nothing is all I feel
Sometimes I wonder
If nothing is something
Or then, I just hope that it is

Body

The skull sits
Peering out of his castle
He commands
His wife the brain
Lounges pulling threads
She directs
Their kingdom the body
Holds up the rest
It persists
In this function of beings
The skull brain and body
They survive

Lightning Flashed and the Rain Poured

My mother read a poem and reminded me of
living
Of how the thunder roars louder on a night
without power
Of how it sounded when she spoke while I lay in
her bosom
Of how I burned at the touch of the curling iron
she held
While she twisted and pulled at my locks
My mother breathed in me life and reminded me
of poetry

Two worlds

I shouldn't	I'm happy to
Have to choose	Whatever you need
Between	There's nobody
Two worlds	Else in my world
But I do	At least
Every day	Not today

Loving Me Is As Dangerous As

Hugging a loaded firecracker
Kissing the end of a hot poker
Standing on the ledge of the Grand Canyon
And looking straight down

It's exciting it's
Burning
It's exhilarating until
Gravity kicks in

Whoops

Mistakes were made
But I'm made of mistakes

Woman

I am woman hear me
scream for frustration at
Man that infuriates
and drives me up the wall

I am woman hear me
moan at Man's touch
in the dark so
soft and heartbreaking gentle

I am woman hear me
cry for Man has left
me again for something
he did not see in me

I am woman hear me
no more for I
am a silent warrior
broken and wise to Man's tricks

I am woman hear me
and listen to my
story and know our
woman needs no Man

Boys Be Like

"I could treat her
so much better"
then does
the same thing

the same thing that
old men do
when they captured
the prize

the prize that they
hang on the wall
without light
in its eyes

In its eyes the
remnants of
what used to be shining
in them

In them is the pride
that they've killed
and not preserved
another prize

another prize
that would be saved
if boys
were not old men

Colors

15

Blue of a peacock
Red of the leaf
Yellow of death
Brown of the buffalo

Bugs in each breath
Buzz of the air
Strain of the muscle
while you carried me there

NoOne

NoOne writes songs about how much it hurts to
break a heart
to fail at being the one that they needed
to want to love as much as you could
but never outliving the lie

NoOne says how much it hurts to hear the one
you broke
screaming at you through the radio
in every breakup song you'll ever hear
swearing and cursing you

NoOne reassures you that it's ok that you've
moved on
even though you called it
even though you caused the most pain

NoOne reminds you that you're not a monster
for choosing yourself
for knowing your own heart,
for wondering if you even have one left to be
whole

NoOne loves you completely

Untitled

I think
I've
lost
my heart
somewhere in
the past
It's cold
in my chest
no
fingerprints of
the thieves
because
I'm the one
that chose
to leave
it
behind
somewhere

somewhere in
the dust

Red Ink

I always thought it was the page that was bleeding but I was wrong I am the one who's life force is dripping I am the one whose pain is preserved in the testament of these words the page and the pen are merely my tools me medical kit my doctor and psychiatrist self prescribed medicine may not be the most effective it certainly adds the illusion of healing isn't that all what life is made of illusions and perceptions what even is truth if all eyes look differently at the world is my red the same as your red does my blood taste the same as your blood is my pain as acute as your pain I only had a red pen today now my thoughts are spilling like my blood and this his how I catch them my bowl is the page my wound self inflicted I'll never bother to stop it all up why keep it from bleeding when it tastes so sweet

man I wish you knew

Man I wish you knew

I wish you knew something broke inside me
then an anvil fell on my shoulders

Even if I wanted to smile it would come out as a
grimace

I wish you knew I cried in the shower
with the fan on
so no one could hear
on my knees bent over to the bottom of the tub

Man I wish you knew when

I was alone in my room searching for relief to
my pain

I wanted to wake you up like I did as a kid and
give you a hug

So you'd give me one back

I don't want to be small
but I don't think
It's bad when you hold me
and I feel like I'm little enough
for you to carry me up and away

Lonely

She was lonely in the way that she graced the
morning
with her long, drawn out stretches,
the way her hair fell once she pulled it out of her
braid,
and the way she smiled right into the mirror
every day,
without even knowing
deep inside
even she could not fool the reflection

Memory

If I could
I'd remember
Every moment of idea

Because then
I'd remember
Every moment worth living

And then
I'd remember
Every gift I'd been given

And then
I'd remember
Myself